Bruce Lee

Wisdom for the Way

Bruce Lee

Wisdom for the Way

Compiled by Shannon Lee

Edited by Sarah Dzida

Graphic Design by Steve Kirwan

Cover Design by Katherine Delaney

Additional Design by John Bodine

©2009 Bruce Lee Enterprises, LLC

All Rights Reserved
Printed in China
Library of Congress Control Number: 2009909072
ISBN-10: 0-89750-185-3
ISBN-13: 978-0-89750-185-9

Tenth Printing 2023

BLACK BELT®
P U B L I S H I N G®
A Division of **BLACK BELT®**
MAGAZINE 1000

*B*ruce Lee ~ *Wisdom for the Way* is a gift. More than a gift book, it is a gift of inspiration. We sought to bring together a book of some of my father's most inspirational and thought-provoking quotes with some beautiful and evocative images so that as you read, you are also uplifted by a visual element. The imagery consists of Bruce Lee photos, graphic elements, and symbolic pictures that are meant to help express the essence of the words on the page.

My father was constantly writing, whether it was penning letters to friends, pondering his own experiences, or researching and taking in the experience of others. He wrote constantly in journals, in the margins of books, and on paper. Writing really helped him process and understand his thoughts and his daily experience. He was also compelled to share these thoughts with friends, co-workers and anyone with a true interest and desire to have a provocative discussion about life. So we are the beneficiaries of all this, for we have a written legacy that, in my father's tradition, we are able to continue to share.

There are many books composed of my father's written words available for sale these days, but we felt it was important to make an accessible and manageable but also beautifully appointed collection of quotes that anyone can pick up, easily flip through and come away affected by its wisdom and beauty. Unlike some of the others, this book is not focused on one specific topic, and it is not of overwhelming length. It is meant to be simple. I hope you enjoy this book and return to it often. I hope you reflect on the words and the images and are as inspired by them as I am every time! This truly is wisdom for the way. ...

Shannon Lee

Empty your mind.

Be formless,
shapeless—like water.

If you put water into a cup,
it becomes the cup.

You put water into a bottle,
it becomes the bottle.

You put it in a teapot,
it becomes the teapot.

Now, water can flow
or it can crash.

Be water, my friend.

Using

no way as way;
having no limitation
as limitation.

The original founder of a style
started out with hypothesis.
But now it has become
the gospel truth,
and people who go into that
become the product of it.
It doesn't matter
how you are,
who you are,
how you are structured,
how you are built
or how you are made…
it doesn't seem to matter.
You just go in there and
be that product.
And that, to me, is not right.

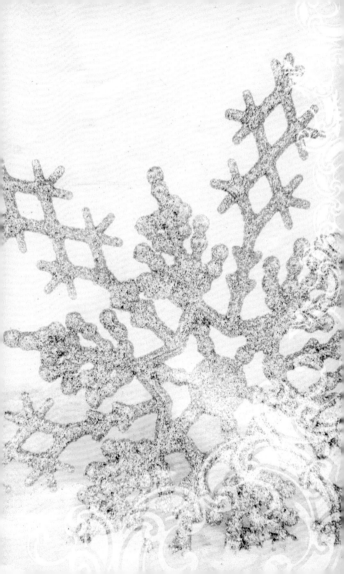

All

types

of

knowledge

ultimately

mean

self-knowledge.

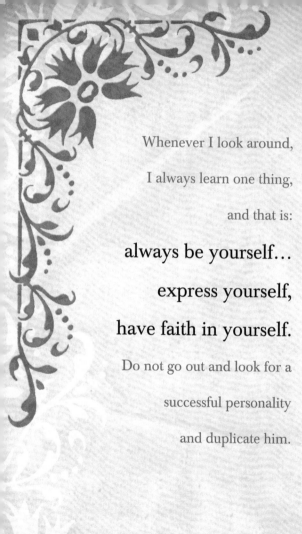

Whenever I look around,

I always learn one thing,

and that is:

always be yourself...

express yourself,

have faith in yourself.

Do not go out and look for a

successful personality

and duplicate him.

To me, ultimately,
martial art means
honestly expressing yourself.
Now it is very difficult to do.
It is easy for me to put on a show
and be cocky and
then feel pretty cool.
Or I can do all kinds
of phony things.
Or I can show you some
really fancy movement.
But to express oneself honestly,
not lying to oneself
—that, my friend,
is very hard to do.

If I tell you I'm good,
probably you will say
that I'm boasting.

But if I tell you
I'm not good,
you'll know I'm lying.

Be pliable.

When a man is living,

he is soft and pliable;

when he is dead,

he becomes rigid.

Pliability is life;

rigidity is death,

whether one speaks

of man's body,

mind or his spirit.

Remember,
success is a journey,
not a destination.

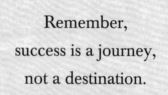

Have faith in your ability.
You will do just fine.

You know how I like

to think of myself?

As a *human being*.

Because, under the sky,

under the heavens,

there is but one family.

It just so happens

people are different.

Willpower:

Recognizing that
the power of will is
the supreme court over
all other departments
of my mind, I will
exercise daily when
I need the urge to act
for any purpose; and
I will form habits
designed to bring the
power of my will
into action at least
once daily.

You have to create
your own luck.
You have to be aware
of the opportunities
around you and
take advantage of them.

Defeat is a state of

no one is ever defeated

until defeat has been accepted

as a reality.

To me, defeat in anything

is merely temporary,

and its punishment is but an urge

for me to exert greater effort

to achieve my goal.

Defeat simply tells me

that something is wrong in my doing;

it is a path leading to

success and truth.

nind;

Once I slow down

because I think

I have reached

my peak,

then my skills

will go nowhere

but down.

Learning

is definitely not mere imitation,

nor is it the ability

to accumulate and regurgitate

fixed knowledge.

Learning

is a constant process of discovery

—a process without end.

Conscience:

Recognizing that my emotions
often err in their over-enthusiasm,
and my faculty of reason
often is without the warmth of feeling
that is necessary to enable me
to combine justice with mercy
in my judgments,
I will encourage my conscience
to guide me as to what is
right and wrong,
but I will never set aside
the verdicts it renders,
no matter what may be
the cost of carrying them out.

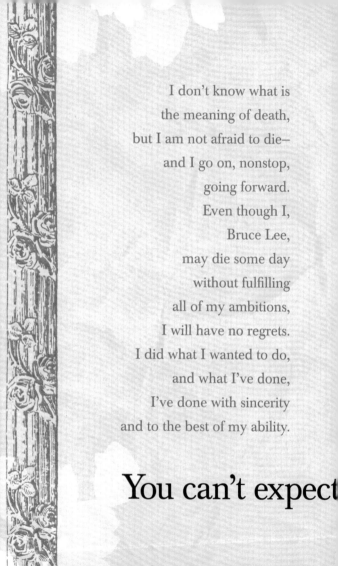

I don't know what is
the meaning of death,
but I am not afraid to die–
and I go on, nonstop,
going forward.
Even though I,
Bruce Lee,
may die some day
without fulfilling
all of my ambitions,
I will have no regrets.
I did what I wanted to do,
and what I've done,
I've done with sincerity
and to the best of my ability.

You can't expect

much more from life.

Art is really

the expression

of the self.

In building a statue,

a sculptor doesn't keep

adding clay to his subject.

Actually, he keeps

chiseling away at

the nonessentials

until the truth of his creation

is revealed without obstruction.

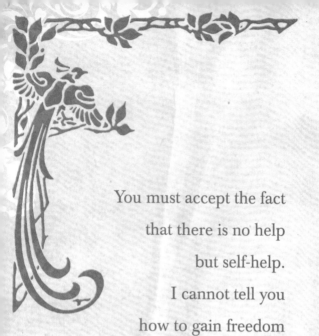

You must accept the fact
that there is no help
but self-help.
I cannot tell you
how to gain freedom
since

freedom exists
within you.

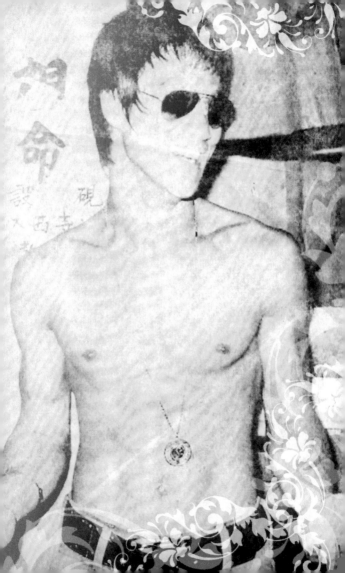

Subconscious Mind:

Reorganizing the influence
of my subconscious mind
over my power of will,
I shall take care to submit to it
a clear and definite picture
of my major purpose in life
and all minor purposes
leading to my major purpose,
and I shall keep this picture
constantly before my
subconscious mind
by repeating it daily!

A martial artist is a

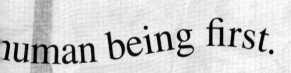

...uman being first.

Just as nationalities have

nothing to do

with one's humanity,

so they have nothing to do

with martial arts.

If nothing within you

        stays rigid,

outward things

will disclose themselves.

    Moving, be like water;

still, be like a mirror;

respond like

        an echo.

The great mistake

is to anticipate

the outcome

of the engagement;

you ought not

to be thinking of

whether it ends

in victory or

in defeat.

Let nature take

its course, and

your tools

will strike at

the right moment.

Memory:

Recognizing the value
of an alert mind and
an alert memory,
I will encourage mine
to become alert by
taking care to impress it clearly
with all thoughts I wish to recall
and by associating
those thoughts
with related subjects
which I may call to mind
frequently.

We shall find
the truth
when we examine
the problem.

The problem is
never apart from
the answer.
The problem *is*
the answer—
understanding
the problem
dissolves
the problem.

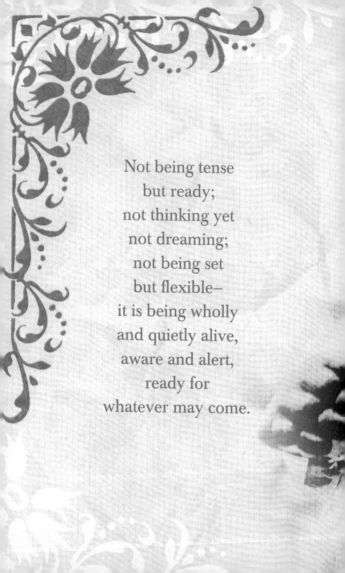

Not being tense
but ready;
not thinking yet
not dreaming;
not being set
but flexible–
it is being wholly
and quietly alive,
aware and alert,
ready for
whatever may come.

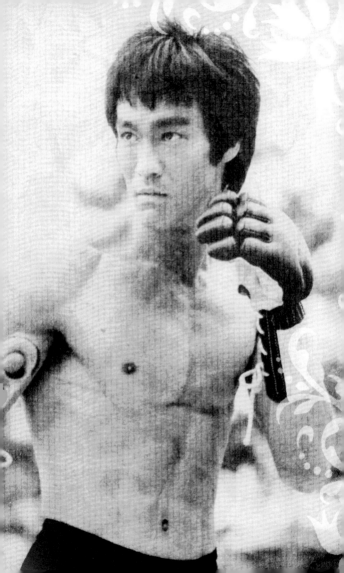

It is compassion
rather than principle of justice
that can guard us against being
unjust to our fellow men.

We are told that

talent creates

its own opportunities.

Yet it sometimes seems

that intense desire

creates not only

its own opportunities

but its own talents

as well.

Self-actualizatior

s the important thing.

And my personal message to people
is that I hope they will go toward
self-actualization rather than
self-image actualization.
I hope that they will search
within themselves for
honest self-expression.

It is like a finger
pointing a way
to the moon.
Don't concentrate
on the finger
or you will miss
all that

heavenly
glory.

Independent inquiry

is needed in your

search for truth,

not dependence

on anyone else's view

or a mere book.

The meaning
of life
is that it is
to be *lived*.

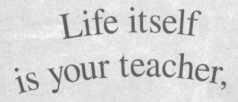

Life itself
is your teacher,

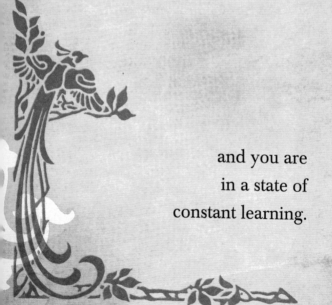

and you are
in a state of
constant learning.

Remember, my friend,
to enjoy your planning
as well as your accomplishment,

for life is
too short for
negative energy.

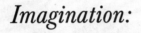

Imagination:

Recognizing the need
for sound plans and ideas
for the attainment of my
desires, I will develop my
imagination by calling
upon it daily for help in
the formation of my plans.

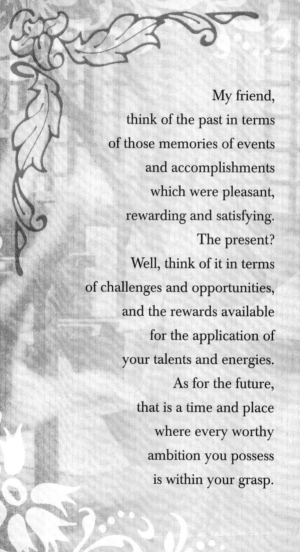

My friend,
think of the past in terms
of those memories of events
and accomplishments
which were pleasant,
rewarding and satisfying.
The present?
Well, think of it in terms
of challenges and opportunities,
and the rewards available
for the application of
your talents and energies.
As for the future,
that is a time and place
where every worthy
ambition you possess
is within your grasp.

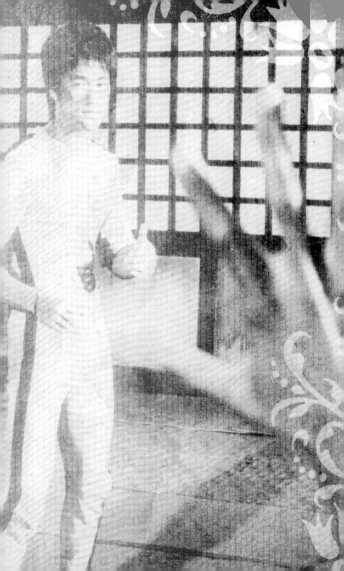

What we are after is the root

and not the branches.

The root is the real knowledge;

the branches are surface knowledge.

Real knowledge breeds "body feel"

and personal expression;

surface knowledge breeds

mechanical conditioning

and imposing limitation and

squelches creativity.

The past is no more;

the future is not yet.

Nothing exists except

the here and now.

Our grand business is

not to see what lies

dimly at a distance,

but to do what lies

clearly at hand.

If you spend
too much time
thinking about
a thing,

**you'll never
get it done.**

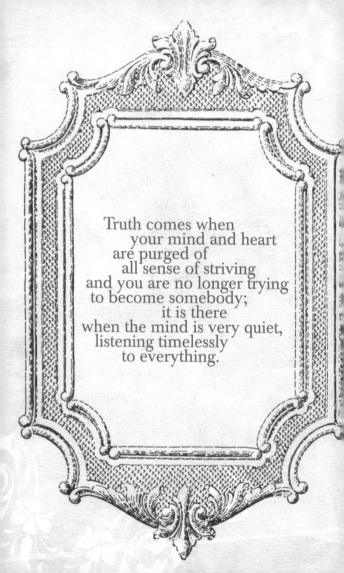

Truth comes when
your mind and heart
are purged of
all sense of striving
and you are no longer trying
to become somebody;
it is there
when the mind is very quiet,
listening timelessly
to everything.

Success means doing

something

sincerely
and
wholeheartedly.

Reason:

Recognizing that my
positive and negative
emotions may be dangerous
if they are not controlled
and guided to desirable ends,
I will submit all my desires,
aims, and purposes to
my faculty of reason,
and I will be guided by it
in giving expression
to these.

Don't
think–

feel!

Knowledge
will give you power,
**but character,
respect.**

Every emotion
expresses itself
in the
muscular system.
Anxiety is
tremendous
excitement held,
bottled up.

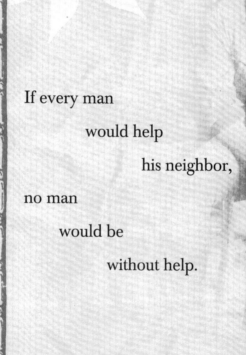

If every man

would help

his neighbor,

no man

would be

without help.

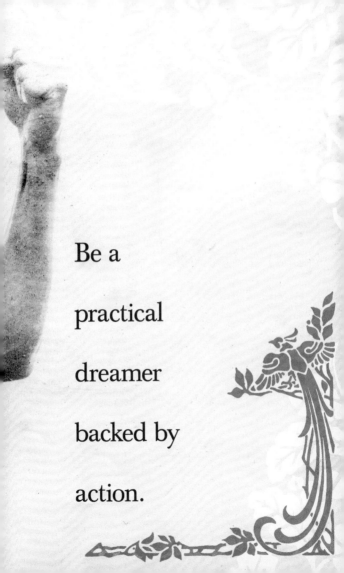

Be a

practical

dreamer

backed by

action.

It is not a shame
to be knocked down
by other people.
The important thing
is to ask when you're
being knocked down,
"Why am I being
knocked down?"

If a person can
reflect in this way,
then there is hope
for the person.

To

change

with

change

is the

changeless

state.

What I honestly value
more than anything else is
quality:
doing one's best
in the manner of
the responsibility and
craftsmanship of a
Number One.

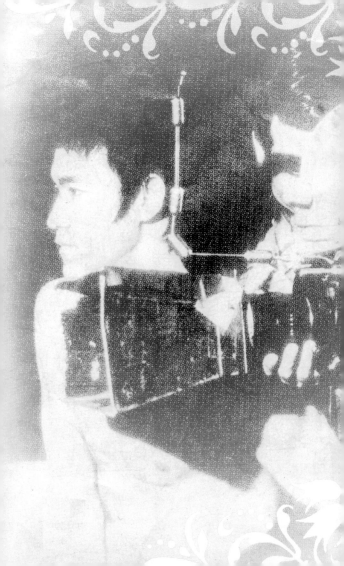

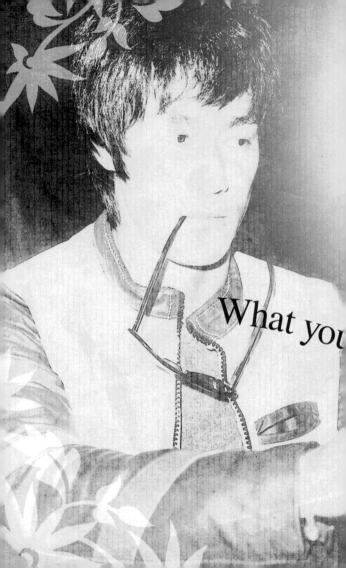

What you

habitually think

largely determines
what you will
ultimately become.

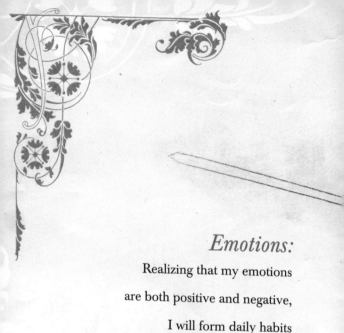

Emotions:

Realizing that my emotions
are both positive and negative,
I will form daily habits
which will encourage
the development of
the positive emotions
and aid me in converting
the negative emotions
into some form of
useful action.

Bruce Lee

A goal is not always

meant to be reached.

It often serves simply as

something to aim at.

Keep your mind on
the things you want
and off those you don't.

You will never get
any more out of life
than you expect.

Every man today
is the result
of his thoughts
of yesterday.

Probably people will say

I'm too conscious of success.

Well, I am not.

Success comes to those who

become success-conscious.

If you don't aim at an object,

how the heck on earth

do you think you can get it?

When I look around,
I always learn something
and that is

to be
always yourself.

And to express
yourself.
To have faith in
yourself.
Do not go out
and look for a
successful personality
and duplicate it …
start from the very root of (your)
being, which is

"how can I be me?"

Research your own

absorb what is useful,

reject what is useless and

add what is essentially

your own.

experience;

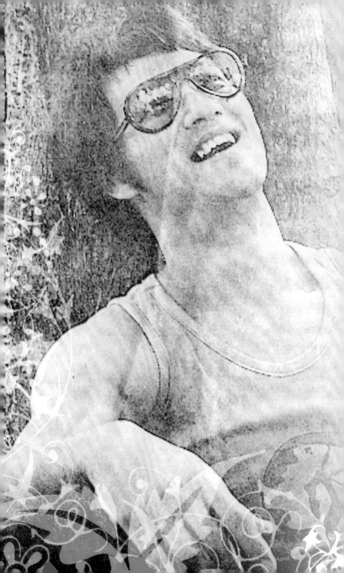

When I have listened
to my mistakes,

I
have
grown.

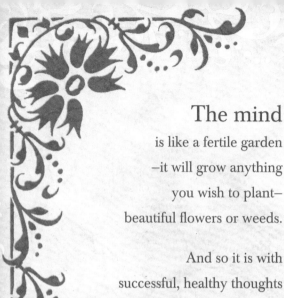

The mind

is like a fertile garden
—it will grow anything
you wish to plant—
beautiful flowers or weeds.

And so it is with
successful, healthy thoughts
or negative ones that will,
like weeds, strangle and
crowd the others.

Do not allow
negative thoughts
to enter your mind
for they are the weeds
that strangle confidence.

We do not live for;
we simply

live.

We are always in the process

of becoming and nothing is fixed.

Have no rigid system in you

and you'll be flexible to

change with the ever-changing.

Open yourself and flow at once

with the total flowing now.

Anger
blinds!

Life is wide,
limitless—

there is no border,
no frontier.

So, action! Action!

Never wasting energy
on worries and
negative thoughts.
I mean who has the
most insecure job
as I have?
What do I live on?
My faith in my ability
that I'll make it.
Sure, my back screwed
me up good for a year,
but with every adversity
comes a blessing
because a shock acts as
a reminder to oneself
that we must not get
stale in routine.
Look at a rainstorm;
after its departure
everything grows!

Be proficient in your field
as well as in

harmony

among fellow men.

What is
true stillness?

Stillness in
movement.

One will never get any more

than he thinks he can get.

You have
what it takes.

Look back and see

your progress—

damn the torpedo,

full speed ahead!

For Further information on Bruce Lee or the art of Jeet
Kune Do®, Please contact:

Bruce Lee Foundation
11693 San Vicente Blvd
Suit #918
Los Angeles, CA 90049

www.bruceleefoundation.org
www.brucelee.com

The Bruce Lee Foundation, a California 501(c)(3) public benefit corporation, seeks to
preserve, perpetuate, and disseminate Bruce Lee's life example, phylosophies, and
art of Jun Fan Jeet Kune Do® through inspirational events, educational programs,
martial arts instruction, and the Bruce Lee Action Mueseum. We beleive that the
Bruce Lee Foundation can enrich lives, open minds and break down barriers through
the active proliferation of Bruce Lee's legacy of undaunted optimism in the face of
adversity, unwavering humanism, mental and physical perseverance, and inspirational presence of mind toward the betterment of our global community.